God at Work
in Brazil

1997-98 NWMS READING BOOKS

RESOURCE BOOK FOR THE LEADER

IMAGINE THE POSSIBILITIES
Edited by Beverlee Borbe

FOR THE READER

BY GRACE TRANSFORMED
God at Work in Brazil
By Tim Crutcher

ONLY ONE LIFE . . .
The Autobiography of Lorraine O. Schultz
By Lorraine O. Schultz with C. Ellen Watts

JESUS WILL REPAY
By Becky Hancock

THAILAND: LAND OF THE WHITE ELEPHANT
Edited by Jean R. Knox and Michael P. McCarty

TO THE SHELTER
Journeys of Faith in the Middle East
By Kay Browning

WHERE THE RIVER FLOWS
Bringing Life to West Africa
By Linda Seaman

By Grace Transformed

God at Work in Brazil

TIM CRUTCHER

NPH

Nazarene Publishing House
Kansas City, Missouri

ISBN 083-411-6448

Printed in the
United States of America

Cover design: Paul Franitza

Photo by: David Pollack

10 9 8 7 6 5 4 3 2 1

Again for Rhonda, whose dedication to me
deserves far more than this dedication can repay.

CONTENTS

Tim Crutcher is the mission education coordinator for the Nazarene World Mission Society. A graduate of Southern Nazarene University and Nazarene Theological Seminary, Tim has authored numerous articles, lessons, and resource pieces for the denomination. He lives with his wife and son in Kansas City.

PREFACE

This is a book about lives by grace transformed. Hopefully in these pages you will glimpse just a small part of the wonderful work God is doing in Brazil through the Church of the Nazarene. But before we get to them, I feel I must give a quick word of explanation, maybe even warning.

Too often, I fear, we sensationalize missions and the gospel by telling only stories of dramatic change. I believe these stories need to be told, or else I would not have written this book. However, these stories are made possible only by the unglamorous sacrifice and often frustrating labor that consume much of a missionary's energy.

It is my prayer that your life will be touched by these transformed lives, that these stories will give you tangible proof that God is at work through your prayers and offerings. But as you read, you might remember that God is at work in the quiet, constant stories of "keeping grace" as much as He is in the dramatic transformations. And I believe the kingdom of God advances as much by steady, smaller, often untold steps as it does by the leaps and bounds represented in this book.

ACKNOWLEDGMENTS

This book would not have been possible without the efforts and initiative of Stephen and Brenda Heap, whose vision for this book brought it into your hands. I also must thank all of the wonderful and gracious Brazilian Nazarenes who let me share their lives. *Não há uma familia como a familia de Deus. Muito Obrigado, Irmãos.*

INTRODUCTION

Aside from having mental pictures of Rio de Janeiro, the Amazon River, large coffee exports, and possibly great soccer players and teams, most people don't know much about Brazil. In fact, many still think that people in Brazil speak Spanish, when Brazil is actually the largest Portuguese-speaking nation in the world. It is an exciting country containing all extremes of climate and geography and just as many extremes of people. It is a land with great natural resources occupied by a people who want to use those resources to become a major player on the world stage. Brazil is also one of the most exciting places in the world to be a part of the Church of the Nazarene.

Although many people may realize that Brazil is the largest country in South America, unless they've seen Brazil on a globe (because most flat map projections exaggerate the size of North America and Europe), they probably don't realize just how big the country is. Brazil is about one "Texas" larger than the continental United States of America, but that great territory has only somewhat over half as many people (which is still not an inconsiderable amount—about 150 million people).

Most of the population of Brazil is concentrated on the eastern seaboard, which leaves great tracts of land, much of it jungle and forest, that are inhabited only by small native Amazonian tribes. In fact, there are places in the interior of Brazil where the Brazilian government has posted signs saying, "Beyond this point, Brazilian law does not apply. This area is governed by tribal law."

Despite the presence of such areas, Brazil is a highly technologically advanced society. São Paulo (reportedly the third-largest city in the world) is an industrial giant with well-developed media and telecommunications industries. Even in what many would call the lowest-class areas of the cities (called favelas in Brazil), you will still find such items as satellite dishes and cellular phones. Many people in Brazil enjoy a high standard of living, and a newly stable economy has brought great hope for the future.

And yet many Brazilians question their government's ability to handle the country well and guide it into a place of leadership in the world community. Though Brazil as a nation is almost 200 years old, the present civilian government has been around for only a little more than 10 years, and they have already impeached one president. Even though both the restoration of civilian government and the impeachment of the president came about because of great popular pressure, most Brazilians still view their government as quite distant from the people.

This combination of hope and uncertainty has created an environment in which the Evangelical church in Brazil has grown very well, the Church of the Nazarene included. In fact, if present trends continue, experts predict that Brazil will be the leading Evangelical nation in the world sometime early in the next century. Yet there is still much work to be done.

The religious background of Brazil, like most countries in Central and South America, is that of colonial Catholicism that many people have mixed with tribal religions, mostly brought from Africa as a result of the slave trade. This mix, often referred to as spiritism, is occultic in nature, though most of its practitioners would not say that they are dealing with the demonic. With such a religion so openly accepted by many people in Brazil, one can easily see the need for the message of heart holiness and the banner of the Church of the Nazarene.

Here, then, are just a few of the stories of those who have been transformed by that message of holiness and who are working to spread that transformation throughout their nation.

Manaus
BRAZIL
Recife
Brasilia
Belo Horizonte
Vitória
Campinas
Rio de Janeiro
Londrina
São Paulo
Curitiba
Florianópolis

1

How Firm a Foundation

Lazaro Aguiar and Campinas Central Church of the Nazarene

LAZARO AGUIAR ALLOWED HIMSELF to be guided to the church building by two young children, each one clutching one of his hands. They seemed to be excited about going to Sunday School. If it was going to be anything like the youth service the night before, Aguiar thought, then I don't see what the big deal is about. Sure, he enjoyed being with the other teenagers, but going to church had never been his idea of a good time.

Aguiar, like many people in Brazil, had grown up in a Catholic home, his being in the interior town of Itau. His parents were Italian immigrants who had come to Brazil after World War II and shared the common hope of such people that one of their boys would become a priest. Aguiar attended the church often and even served as an altar boy as a young teen, but he never considered it for a career. Granted, those Catholic services weren't much like the service at this Church of the Nazarene he had attended last night, but neither one held much interest for him.

So why was he letting these two children guide him to church?

Aguiar had come to the city of Campinas, Brazil, to escape the authority of his parents and the moral strictures of his Catholic upbringing. Christians, it seemed, just didn't know how to have fun. Since he was 18, he decided to get away to study what he wanted (business administration) and do what he wanted (play soccer). He found a boardinghouse that would take him in, and his life pretty much revolved around himself.

The lady who ran the boardinghouse was something of an odd bird in Aguiar's mind. She attended church quite often, an Evangelical church new to Brazil called the Church of the Nazarene. She actually seemed to enjoy it. Last week she had told him that this church was having a service especially for teenagers in the new building they had just constructed. The service would be boring, Aguiar knew, but he would have a chance to meet some new people and maybe even play some Ping-Pong afterward. So he had decided to go.

And now he found himself going back.

When the landlady's two kids knocked on his door that morning, he was already up. Seeing the cute, eager looks in their eyes, he decided that there would be no harm in accepting their invitation to go to Sunday School with them. After all, he had nothing else planned for that morning.

Again, the service wasn't what Aguiar would have considered interesting, but there was something about it that intrigued him. The next week he found himself going back again. This he continued to do for the next six months.

* * *

It was February 1964. Summer was waning, and Aguiar found himself looking forward to that all-important Brazilian pre-Lenten festival called Carnival, though for different reasons than he often had in the past. This year Aguiar would be attending a Carnival camp with some of his new friends. The camp was sponsored by the new church he had been attending. Of course, he would miss out on the other, more typically Brazilian Carnival activities. But then, Aguiar thought, that was probably why the church held these camps. Apparently these Nazarenes did not approve of what went on during Carnival.

Personally, Aguiar couldn't understand that. Sure, attending church was nice, but it didn't have much to do with the rest of life. At least, that was what Aguiar thought before he went to the camp.

Aguiar was able to maintain his carefree attitude about camp for the first few days, but then it began to get difficult. He managed to avoid most of the services, but the ones he attended gripped his heart. Finally, at the last service of the camp, Aguiar surrendered to the gentle pull of the Holy Spirit and accepted Christ as his Savior.

When Aguiar returned from camp, he went straight back to his home in Itau. There he shared with his Roman Catholic family this new life he had found in Christ.

"What do you mean you've become an Evangelical?" Aguiar's father's voice conveyed both disappointment and betrayal. "We raised you to be a good Catholic. We even wanted you to be a priest, and now you've gone over to the side of the enemy. Well, if that's the way you're going to be, you can expect nothing from us. In fact, you'd better leave just as soon as you can."

Aguiar's mother did not say much, but he could tell she shared her husband's feelings.

With nothing else to say, Aguiar turned and walked out the door. It hurt him deeply that his family would not accept his decision to follow Christ, but Aguiar had committed himself to this journey regardless of other people's reaction. Forging ahead, he enrolled himself at the Nazarene seminary there in Campinas to prepare for a lifetime of ministry.

* * *

At the 1968 graduation ceremonies for the Seminario Teologico Nazareno Brasileiro, Lazaro Aguiar scanned the crowd. He hoped to see his parents somewhere, but deep in his heart he knew they wouldn't be coming. It was too much of an embarrassment for them to have a son who was an Evangelical pastor, much less be caught at an Evangelical graduation.

Aguiar was disappointed at his parents' absence but was not going to let that get him down. There were too many others in attendance who had meant so much to him during these past four years at the seminary. He looked over to where the professors were sitting and saw Charles and Roma Gates. Those two had shaped Aguiar's thinking and faith through their teaching, and he would always be grateful to them.

Just down from the Gateses were the Mostellers. Earl Mosteller, Aguiar knew, would always be the model for him of a man of prayer. During all-night prayer vigils, Dr. Mosteller had been known to pray for four hours without stopping. Aguiar smiled as he wondered, not for the first time, where he came up with all those subjects to talk to God about.

Aguiar's smile remained on his face as his gaze shifted to the two people who had had the greatest impact on him during his seminary career—Jim and Carol Kratz. The Kratzes had come to pastor the Campinas Central Church of the Nazarene after Aguiar had been there for three months. Pastor Kratz had spent hours with Aguiar, discipling him, mentoring him, and teaching him the Scriptures. In Aguiar's mind, Jim Kratz would always represent to him what it really meant to be a pastor.

Aguiar loved Pastor Kratz like a father, so he was glad that he would be able to keep up a relationship with him. After graduation, Aguiar would be moving to Rio de Janeiro, where Pastor Kratz was planting a new church, to serve as an associate. Aguiar found himself looking forward to the move immensely.

When his name was called, Aguiar went to receive his diploma. As he sat down, he thought how much he liked the city of Campinas, and how he wished that someday he might return. But, of course, such things were to be left in God's hands.

* * *

Twelve years after graduation from seminary, God's hands were still guiding. Pastor Lazaro Aguiar began his newest assignment with no small amount of fear and trepidation. He had served two other senior pastorates in important places, first in Rio de Janeiro, then in Belo Horizonte. But neither assignment felt as weighty as this one. Sure, the congregation was only 115 members, but it was a very influential congregation. Pastoring the mother church of the Church of the Nazarene in Brazil was not something to be taken lightly.

In 1958 Earl and Gladys Mosteller decided to begin the Church of the Nazarene in the university town of Campinas, because they thought they could have a greater impact in a smaller city like that than in a major city like São Paulo or Rio de Janeiro. In Campinas there were students from all over Brazil, and if they could tap that resource, it might open the doors to planting the Church of the Nazarene in many other areas of the country.

Despite any reservations he had in pastoring the church in which he himself had been nurtured, Pastor Aguiar threw himself into the task with all the strength and vision God had given him. If this was going to be a church others looked to, Aguiar thought, then I want it to be a church that demonstrates the kingdom of God in action. With that thought in mind, Aguiar went to work.

For the next several years Pastor Aguiar challenged his congregation with the full implications of the gospel. He challenged them to be salt and light in their communities. And he challenged them to reach out beyond their communities with their prayers and their offerings. And so they did, and God began to grow the church.

In just two years, Campinas Central Church outgrew its facility. They remodeled the building, but soon that wasn't enough. They added a Monday night service, but even that was insufficient. The church membership was doubling every year, and the building could not keep up.

As Pastor Aguiar reflected on the problem, he decided that it was a good problem to have. Still, it had to be dealt with. At first he and the church board had begun to plan another remodeling project, but a group of businessmen from the United States had encouraged them to think about another plan.

The Arizona Nazarene Land Investments (ANLI) group came down to dedicate a church that they had helped finance in another part of Brazil. It was obvious to Aguiar that the ANLI group had caught a vision of what could be accomplished by the Church of the Nazarene in Brazil. They were sharing that vision with others in the United States, and they had some sound advice for the Campinas congregation—move.

At first the idea of moving the church met with some resistance. After all, Aguiar smiled to himself, to some people the Campinas church was like Mecca. But the idea had great merit. Two of the ANLI businessmen had helped them scout out the possibilities, since real estate was their business. Now they had found an abandoned factory building that would give them 10 times the space they had before and was situated in an ideal area for growth. God seemed to have His hand on the matter.

Pastor Aguiar and the Campinas church board approached the owner of the new property about the possibility of selling it. The owner of the property wanted U.S.$2 million for it, but he would agree to a trade of properties if the church would pay him $1 million. After four months of negotiation, the church was able to trade the properties without paying anything additional, and the owner even agreed to pay them $150,000.

Knowing that this was the will of God for the Campinas congregation, Pastor Aguiar and the board closed the deal. They knew that there would be much work to do in the months and years ahead, but they were excited about the new possibilities God had given them.

* * *

It was a pleasant summer afternoon in January 1996 when Pastor Aguiar returned to the church from the mayor's office. In the almost 16 years he had been at Campinas Central Church of the Nazarene, praying with the mayor was one of the most interesting experiences he had had. The mayor had been diagnosed with a terminal illness. He had asked Aguiar to come and pray with him after hearing from one of Aguiar's parishioners, a nurse who attended him. Aguiar went to the mayor's office, and the mayor suspended the staff meeting in session so that he could pray. It was quite a moment.

It is nice to serve in a church that is so respected in the community, Aguiar thought as he walked through the main front gate into the stone courtyard. The members of the Campinas congregation, now numbering over 2,000, were known around the city as responsible and upright people. Still, Campinas Central Church of the Nazarene was much more than just a respected institution. It was an institution committed to making a difference.

Going into the church building, Pastor Aguiar walked by the sign for the Jim Kratz Institute, a private Christian school with over 500 students. The church also operates a school for underprivileged kids in a poorer section of town. This school has over 300 students and provides them with education, food, medical care, and most important, the gospel.

Pastor Caleb stopped Aguiar in the hall to ask him a question about his weekly meeting. Pastor Caleb was himself a former drug addict and had suffered serious damage in his brain before the Lord got ahold of him at Campinas Central. Now he directs a ministry to 70 recovering addicts, lectures in public schools about the effects of drugs, and shares his testimony.

Aguiar arrived at his office to the usual stack of papers and notes of phone calls to return. He had to finish his Sunday sermon, check on the plans for the Carnival camps, and make sure all his arrangements were made for him to attend the General Board meeting in Kansas City the next month. And those were just the things on his personal schedule.

Like many pastors in churches with broad ministries, Aguiar sometimes found it very hard to keep up. That happens, Aguiar thought, with a growing church. The church was growing so well that they had planted 15 other churches in the last 12 years and had given away over 400 people in just the last 2 years to start other churches. And with 80 people in the church studying for the ministry, more church plants were already being planned.

And then there were all the other ministries in which church members were involved—the bookstore they ran, the seminary extension program they conducted, the children and youth camps for the Carnival season, and the list just goes on. Aguiar was thankful that God was overseeing it all, because there was no way he could control it. Nor would he want to.

This is how it goes, Aguiar thought as he looked around the office. From tiny seeds and dedicated investments, the church has grown into a strong presence of holiness and grace in the community. And as God prospers it, growth is enabled elsewhere. This is how the gospel should be, Aguiar thought as he took a seat. And this was only one church of many in Brazil with such a vision. With that joyful thought, he found the strength to tackle the daunting mound of paperwork.

2

Shall We Gather at the River

Amadeu Teixeira's Story

AMADEU SMILED AND WAVED to the prison guard as he made his way into the building, pausing first to wipe the mud off his bare feet. The guard nodded in response. Amadeu's father worked for the police force, and that was probably the only reason they let him visit the prisoners. Still, it wasn't as if the guards were worried about him. After all, what harm could the small 12-year-old kid do in a small jail in a small town deep in the interior of Minas Gerais? He didn't even have enough money to buy decent shoes.

Amadeu made a few deliveries of fruit and cookies to some prisoners before pulling up his now familiar seat in front of one specific, special cell. It was his usual spot, and it afforded him the most enjoyable hours of his day.

Amadeu had no idea what João had done to land himself in prison, but he figured it couldn't have been all that bad. Amadeu's father had regularly beat him for what seemed to be the smallest of offenses, so he could imagine that it wouldn't take much for the police to throw someone in jail. Though he was still young and not well acquainted with the adult world, Amadeu had learned that it was not a fair one. He had learned much about suffering and pain since he first came to the prison, but that's what made him keep coming back.

Amadeu had a passion to help people. When he first started going to the prison, it was more out of curiosity than anything else. Now it was out of a sense of compassion that wouldn't let him do otherwise. When he was younger, he had dreamed about becoming a priest. Now he dreamed about becoming a policeman so he could really help people, especially people like these, and treat them the way they should be treated.

"Good morning," he called to the cell's occupant.

"Good morning, Amadeu," the prisoner replied with a smile, a smile that seemed more pronounced than normal.

"You seem to be quite happy today," Amadeu said, making conversation as he set up the domino board for their daily game.

"I am," came the simple reply. Amadeu gave the prisoner a questioning look. "I'm going home today," the man said after a brief silence.

Amadeu was stunned. The domino pieces dropped from his hands. Obviously they wouldn't be playing today, nor ever again. In the months since João had arrived, he and Amadeu had developed a close friendship during Amadeu's daily visits. Although he was glad that João was being released, deep down inside Amadeu didn't want him to go.

The prisoner could see the disappointment on the young man's face through the bars. He turned and looked around the room. Aside from a few old clothes with patches, his only possession was a book. After only a moment's hesitation, he picked it up and turned back to Amadeu.

"You've been a real friend to me, Amadeu," he began. "You've helped my days in this place to pass much more quickly than they would have otherwise. I want to give you something, but I don't have much myself."

He handed Amadeu the book through the bars. Amadeu mutely accepted it. "I want you to have this," the prisoner went on. "I know you've been studying in school, and I know you can read it. You ought to. It will help you like no other book I know."

That night, after he had gone to draw water from the well and finished his other chores, Amadeu took up the book. With the aid of a small olive oil and string lamp, he leafed through its pages with only minimal interest. There were no pictures, and the words seemed hard to understand. Amadeu put the book onto a small shelf near his bed beside a small, crude statue. Seeing the statue, he offered up a quick prayer to St. Judas Tadeu and then blew out the lamp. The book remained untouched on that shelf until one day Amadeu's grandmother came for a visit.

Amadeu's grandmother was what his father termed an "Evangelical." Amadeu didn't know what an Evangelical was supposed to be, but from the way his father and the priest talked about them, they couldn't be very good. Still, Grandmother was allowed to come for a visit, so Evangelicals couldn't be that bad either.

As always, when Grandmother arrived, she conducted a thorough examination of the house. No one was ever quite sure what she was looking for, because she never seemed to find it; but in that search she came across Amadeu's book.

"Amadeu," she began sternly, "don't you know that it is a sin to treat the Bible this way?"

Amadeu, having no idea what a Bible was, couldn't understand how it could be a sin to leave it on the shelf.

"This is the Word of God," his grandmother continued. Then her eyes became softer. "Can you read, Amadeu?"

"Yes, Grandmother," Amadeu replied, grateful for a question he could answer.

"I want you to read some of this Book to me."

And so Amadeu began to read the Bible, out loud to his grandmother at first, then silently to himself after she left. The more he read, the deeper the Book spoke to him. He began to underline passages that spoke to him. It did not take long for young Amadeu to become convinced of the truth of this Book, and so he accepted as his Lord and Savior this Jesus of whom the Book spoke.

Amadeu wanted to attend an Evangelical church in the town where he lived, but his father forbade him to go. He could hardly tolerate the fact that his son had become an Evangelical, and he certainly wasn't going to encourage it by letting him hang around with others. Amadeu could go to Catholic mass all he wanted, but an Evangelical church was out of the question.

Amadeu accepted the authority of his father with patience. He continued to read his Bible and talk with other Evangelicals whenever he got the chance. One day, when Amadeu was 16, his father caught him talking to a young Evangelical lady. That day Amadeu received the harshest beating of his life, and through that beating he learned something. He decided that God must be on the side of these Evangelicals, teaching them what was good and right, for his father to be so violently opposed to them. Surely God could not be on the side of someone who would beat his son so severely.

That incident renewed Amadeu's determination to live out and spread this new life he had found. Since his father did not stop him from reading the Bible, he continued to read voraciously, finishing the entire book once a year. He began to read the book to his eight brothers and even preached to them from it. He attended the masses of the local Catholic church in the morning, and in the evening he would read late into the night.

One Sunday morning, completely without warning, Amadeu's father decided that the whole family would attend the Evangelical church in town. After attending once, he decided that it wasn't so bad after all, and he let Amadeu attend whenever he wanted. This Amadeu did faithfully for several years.

God had given Amadeu a good job, and with his money he had built a new house for the family just behind the church he was attending near the edge of town. Now that he lived so close, the pastor began to ask for his help in the church. The pastor was a very devout but very simple man who had never had time to learn to read or speak well. He asked Amadeu to help with the services, to read the Bible, and even occasionally to preach.

Amadeu found himself enjoying this work with the church. He enjoyed it so much that he wanted to learn more so that he could help more. Since there was no seminary in town, Amadeu began to look for a correspondence course. Reading through an Evangelical magazine, he found two such courses. He ordered them both, looked them over, and then decided on the one that looked better to him. That was 1967.

A year and a half later a stranger walked into the church where Amadeu was assisting, a stranger whom God would use to change his life. The stranger arrived while Amadeu was directing some choruses. The pastor went to greet him, learned that he was a pastor, and asked him, as was customary, if he wanted to preach. The stranger quickly agreed and took a seat on the platform.

When Amadeu finished directing the choruses, he took a seat next to this stranger. The stranger asked him to read the text for the sermon. Amadeu agreed, though inside he kept wondering what sort of pastor this stranger was. He feared that he might be a Mormon or a member of some odd cult, but his fears were quickly allayed after he heard the sermon.

After church, Amadeu's father invited the stranger to their house, since it was so close to the church. There they learned how he had come to this small town in the interior of Brazil. He had come by mistake.

This pastor, whose name they learned was Pastor Jim Kratz, had been trying to visit some people who had moved from his church in Rio de Janeiro to the interior city of Montes Claros. Somehow he found himself more than 100 miles off course. Since it was Sunday, he decided to find a service to attend and so wound up at Amadeu's church.

As they talked, Amadeu noticed that Pastor Kratz was paying special attention to him. He seemed to be reading Amadeu with his eyes. When the conversation got back to the morning's service, Amadeu found out the reason for this.

"You've got a nice voice, Son," Pastor Kratz told him. "And you read well. You ought to consider going to seminary."

"I am studying in a correspondence program, sir," Amadeu answered helpfully. He noticed Pastor Kratz's eyes brighten.

"Which one?"

Amadeu went back into his room and got his books. As he handed them to Pastor Kratz, the man appeared as if he were going to faint. He shook his head, and then his face broke out into a great smile. Everyone was looking at him, wondering what it was about the books that caused this reaction, when he flipped to the back of one of the books and showed a picture to Amadeu. It was a picture of Pastor Kratz. The books were from the Nazarene seminary in Campinas, and Pastor Kratz was a Nazarene.

At once Amadeu knew that God had sent Pastor Kratz his way. Pastor Kratz knew it too. When he left, he gave Amadeu some other books and told him that they would meet again soon. That meeting occurred six months later, in June 1969. Amadeu was invited to Campinas to attend the Nazarene district assembly because he was one of the best students in the correspondence program. The church would pay all his expenses. For Amadeu, it would be the first time he had ever been outside his home state.

The assembly gave Amadeu an opportunity to get to know these Nazarenes better, and he liked what he saw. After the assembly was over, Pastor Kratz invited him to come back to Rio de Janeiro with him and see the work there. Amadeu accepted.

Jim Kratz was living in the Mesquita area of Rio while pastoring in Nilopolis. At that time there was no church in Mesquita, but the Kratzes were looking to start one. While Amadeu was there, he had the opportunity to preach to a small group of people gathered in the Kratzes' living room.

Amadeu returned to his hometown confident that God had called him to preach. He then made preparations to move to Campinas and study in the Nazarene seminary there full-time. As Amadeu readied himself for this move, Pastor Kratz sent him an intriguing letter.

The letter was an invitation to join the Kratzes in Rio and help with the ministry there. They wanted to start a church in the Mesquita area, and they felt God was calling Amadeu to help them. In Rio, Amadeu would get good, hands-on experience in ministry, and he could still study through the seminary's extension program there.

Amadeu desperately wanted to go to Rio to help Pastor Kratz, but he knew that if he did so, he would have to join with these Nazarenes once and for all. Before he made that step, he determined to talk to his pastor.

Amadeu's pastor, being a simple man of simple faith, simply said, "Who am I to argue with the Lord's calling? We will miss you, Amadeu. We will miss your work, and," he added with a wry smile, "we will miss your tithe. But I know that God has commanded you, so go and be a blessing for the Nazarenes." With the assurance of that affirmation, Amadeu bid his family good-bye and packed his belongings for Rio.

Amadeu moved in with the Kratzes in early 1970. They rented a room and began services in Mesquita with 18 people. After just eight months, the Kratzes had to return to the United States for furlough, and Amadeu was made the senior pastor.

Twenty-six years later, Amadeu Teixeira is still the only pastor the Mesquita church has ever known. Many of those original 18 members have gone on to heaven. Some are still in the congregation today, and that original congregation has been multiplied a hundred times over. The church is now the center of one of the two districts in the state of Rio de Janeiro, and Pastor Amadeu serves as the district superintendent.

People who ask Amadeu about his journey from the poverty of his boyhood to the pastorate of one of the largest Churches of the Nazarene in

Brazil all receive the same answer. Pastor Amadeu smiles and reminds them of what the apostle Paul said in 1 Corinthians:

> But God chose the foolish things of the world to shame the wise; God chose the weak things of the world to shame the strong. He chose the lowly things of this world and the despised things—and the things that are not—to nullify the things that are. . . . Therefore, as it is written: "Let him who boasts boast in the Lord" *(1:27-28, 31).*

"God was the One who put shoes on my feet," Pastor Amadeu says. "Everything that has happened to me has been because of God. Now we have the opportunity to put the shoes of the gospel of peace on people throughout Brazil. That is why I came to Rio in the first place. And that is why I stay."

And Pastor Amadeu continues to reach out with the vision God has given him. In addition to operating numerous ministries in the area surrounding Rio, the Mesquita church has reached out all over Brazil. In towns as far away as Fortaleza and São Luis on the Caribbean coast to Campo Grande in the Southwest, members from the Mesquita church have gone out and planted new churches. Other projects are under way in places as far away as Manaus, a city in the Amazon jungle over 1,800 miles from Rio, and the Sertão, an arid and poor area of northeast Brazil.

Most of these new works have been started by people who caught Pastor Amadeu's vision of evangelism and were sent out by God—sometimes by job transfer, sometimes by just picking up and going—to bring His gospel to new areas of Brazil. And their prayer is that these new churches will send out other people to start still more churches.

Pastor Amadeu dreams of the day when the gospel will be preached to all of Brazil. In the meantime, he continues to shepherd his flock, guide his district, and give God all the glory and praise.

3

Thy Dross to Consume and Thy Gold to Refine

The Story of Antonio Leão

PASTOR TONI SURVEYED the Sunday evening crowd in his church in the Jabaquara area of São Paulo, Brazil, a cosmopolitan city of 13 to 18 million people, depending on who's counting. It was a warm, late summer evening, and the February rains were drumming on the roof. Even so, the loud roars of jets landing at the nearby airport could be heard over the patter of raindrops. People lingered in the church, in no hurry to leave because there was no other place they would rather be.

Pastor Toni and some of the men from his church had just prayed with a young man who wanted to receive Jesus as his Savior. The young man had been a drunk, and the Thursday before had been the first time he had ever entered a church. Though tonight he was quite sober, his eyes still reflected the red and rheumy effects of alcohol. But there was a smile on his face. Here was a new creature in Christ, the second one today.

That morning an older man recently released from prison had come to the church, seeking some way to put his life back together. He found people who treated him like a real person and not just like an outcast. He found a family willing to help him and do what they could to get him back on his feet. He also found Christ.

Toni smiled as he reflected on the nine months he had been in this church. The church had grown from a small group of 15 or so core people to an attendance of about 50. People were finding the Lord, those who already knew Him were deepening their walk, and through it all the kingdom of God was marching on.

Though he never thought he would be able to say it, Toni was happy in São Paulo. Not that life was always easy and comfortable in this urban jungle that he and his young family called home. But then, Toni had learned that one's happiness doesn't depend so much on comfort as being in the will of God.

* * *

Antonio José de Castro Leão was raised in a devout Catholic family in Natal, Brazil, the fifth of nine children. When Toni was a teenager back in 1978, his father, a widely known veterinarian in the city, had a personal encounter with Christ while studying the Bible. He joined a group of other like-minded Catholics, and this led to his excommunication from the Roman Catholic Church.

In another part of Natal, Jim and Carol Kratz, Nazarene missionaries, followed with interest the news of this charismatic Catholic group. They, however, had their own problems to contend with. Their dog was sick.

Being a practical man, Jim Kratz was not fond of the idea of spending money to treat a sick dog. However, when it seemed that something had to be done or else the dog would die, Jim finally relented and took the dog in their Volkswagen van. Knowing the name of only one veterinarian in the city, he headed to the clinic of the man whose excommunication had been so widely covered by the local press. And so the Leão family became acquainted with the Church of the Nazarene.

Just a few months later, Toni's father was sharing Christ with him during an evening together in the home. That night both Toni and his sister Anna accepted Christ as their personal Savior. After Toni's conversion, missionary Jim Kratz took a special interest in this young man. Jim connected Toni with a Baptist group in town so that he would have a chance to be fed spiritually with people his own age. It was in that youth group that Toni met a lovely young lady named Lili.

Toni's life began to change dramatically. He quit his study of accounting in the university and began to search for Christ's direction in his life. During an all-night prayer vigil at the church, he accepted God's call on his life to full-time ministry. From that time on, Jim Kratz spent hours with Toni, counseling him, guiding him, and helping him get established in his Christian walk and ministerial identity.

The bond between Toni and the Kratzes grew so strong that when it came time for the Kratzes to go on furlough, Toni was able to accompany them to the United States. There he met a lay couple, Abe and Marjorie Ellis, who offered to help him attend Northwest Nazarene College (NNC) in Nampa, Idaho, and to let him live in their home in Nampa. While there he kept up a long-distance relationship with Lili.

Toni had been attending NNC for only four months when he was forced to make a choice that would determine the course of his future ministry. His father was gravely ill. Jim Kratz called Toni with the news and wondered what Toni would do. Jim knew that other Brazilians had gone to the United States with the intention of returning and then never did. He was afraid that something like that might happen to Toni as well. But he also knew that if Toni came home to be with his father, it would probably mean not being able to return to the United States to finish his education.

Toni made the choice to return home. By the time he arrived on July 4, 1983, his father, who had been in intensive care, was already feeling better. They discussed Toni's future, and Toni's father recommended that he enroll in the Nazarene seminary in Campinas, Brazil, just north of São Paulo.

After Toni had spent a semester at the Seminario Teologico Nazareno Brasileiro, he and Lili were wed. The three and a half years they spent in Campinas were times of real growth for them but also real struggle. For a period of time, Toni even considered finding another denomination, but through the encouragement of missionary Elton Wood, the Lord confirmed his place in the Church of the Nazarene. God used the struggles as a time of growth for both Toni and his wife. During this time He also blessed them with a daughter, Camila.

When the Leãos graduated from seminary, they had five offers for various churches throughout Brazil. There were really only two places in Brazil where they did not want to go: Recife, which was too close to their families; and São Paulo, which was Brazil's largest (and busiest) city.

Missionary Terry Read had given them a standing invitation to Recife while they were still in seminary, but they had no interest in moving to that city. The offer from a church near Campinas seemed to be the one that interested them the most, so they accepted it, only to have the door abruptly closed. Having already declined the other invitations, they were left without a place of ministry.

With nothing else to do, they moved back to Natal to live with one or the other of their parents. After a month and a half of living and trying to find work there, the district superintendent of the Northeast, João Arthur Scuza, came to Toni with a proposition.

"I have a church in the city of Recife," he said, "that some people have started, but it has never taken off. There are only a few attenders, and the district is not able to help you with a salary; but I'd like you to consider whether or not this could be the Lord's will for you."

Given such a seemingly bleak proposal, Toni and Lili went to prayer. They decided that it was the Lord's will for them to work in Recife, and so they made the 200-mile journey to their new home.

Because they had no money, they could not afford to move their furniture to the rooms off the church that served as the parsonage. They arrived with just their mattresses and a stove with which to cook their food. They didn't even have a refrigerator. They were encouraged, however, because they knew they were where God wanted them to be.

Jobs were hard to find in Recife in those days, and the Leão family found themselves in deeper and deeper straits. The work with the church was going well, and missionaries Brian and Beryl Adams were a tremendous encouragement to them; but they could not find adequate means of financial support.

Toni tried his hand at a job that his brother-in-law had given him, selling designer clothing door-to-door, but he discovered that he didn't have the heart to be a salesman and could not make any money at it. After five months in Recife, the situation grew almost desperate.

Both Toni and Lili had grown up in families who, though not rich, were certainly comfortable. Need was a new experience for them, and the lessons it taught them were harsh. They still did not have money to move their furniture and were still surviving with only a stove and mattresses on the floor. They had a hard time keeping milk for young Camila, because they had no refrigerator. They often had to go without food.

They could have talked to their family about their needs, but they felt reluctant to do so. They had not even told the church about their plight. Finally they were down to their last eight dollars.

They had only a little bread left, so Toni told his wife that he was going to the store to buy some bread. Lili told him, "Don't buy the bread. Buy gas for the stove instead. God will provide us the bread." Encouraged by his wife's faith, Toni did just that.

When he returned, he locked himself in an empty room in the house and began to pray and read the Word. As Toni cried out to God and affirmed His faithfulness, the Lord showed him the story of the widow who helped Elijah and whose jug of oil and jar of flour never ran dry.

Toni shared with his wife the word the Lord had given him, and they were both overwhelmed with the presence of the Holy Spirit. Though they had no food and no money, the Lord had given them a profound peace and happiness. Toni went to take a shower, but he told his wife, "Watch carefully, because God is going to supply our needs."

While Toni was in the shower, he heard the honk of a car horn outside. After getting dressed, he emerged to find his sister Anna waiting for him. She didn't really know why she was there, only that she had become so uncomfortable sitting at home that she had to go out. Looking at Toni, she said without preamble, "You have no money, do you?"

It wasn't really a question. Knowing he could not lie, Toni replied that it was true.

They talked for a little while, then Anna wrote out a check and left it with them. It was enough money not only for bread but for groceries for the next two weeks. Toni and Lili began to praise the Lord with great joy.

That night, Toni felt led to tell the people at prayer meeting about how the Lord had marvelously provided for them. The people were amazed. They had no idea their pastor was going through such hardship because they thought he was receiving a salary from the mission. The next day a lady from the church arrived at their house with several bags of groceries. It was so much that they decided to share the groceries with some of their poor neighbors, since the food would spoil without a refrigerator in which to keep it. This resulted in even more contacts for the church.

That day was the turning point for the Leãos' ministry. Just a few weeks after that experience, Toni was given a job teaching English to schoolchildren, a job he had applied for six months before. The church began to grow, and the people in the church began to support Toni and his family financially. Within a year they were able to ask him to quit his secular job and devote his full energies to the church.

Meanwhile other people, even ones outside the denomination, began to send money or provide food. These contacts resulted in further growth in the church and conversions to Christ. The Lord gave the Leãos the promise that they would never again be in want and that their pantry would always be full. They had been faithful to the Lord, and the Lord was demonstrating His faithfulness to them.

The miracles at Recife were not finished for the Leão family, but unfortunately neither were the testings. One night Camila developed a severe fever that would not go away. Though they had no health insurance or money for a doctor, they knew they had to do something. As they were carrying their daughter to the closest hospital, the Adamses happened to drive by and offered to take them to a better hospital. When a group of people from the church heard about Camila's plight, they got together and offered to pay all the medical bills.

During Lili's second pregnancy, she developed severe lower intestinal problems in her ninth month. The pain was very great, and the doctor said they had no choice but to perform surgery, even though such a surgery would endanger the baby's life. Not knowing what to do, Toni and Lili went back home and began to pray. Though Lili was in great pain, she cried out to the Lord, affirmed His power, and asked for a miracle.

That night Lili slept as she had never slept before. When she awoke, she knew God had healed her. She felt so good that she got up and cleaned the house. Toni rejoiced with his wife but still decided to take her to a doctor. The doctor could only agree with amazement that a miracle had indeed been performed. In fact, God had healed her so well that she was able to deliver the child naturally instead of having the cesarean section that the doctors had previously told her was necessary. The Christian doctor who delivered young Margore didn't charge any fee, and a man whom the Leãos had never met gave them two blank checks to cover the rest of the hospital expenses.

As the people saw how the Lord took care of Pastor Toni and his family, it increased their own faith. It proved to them the benefits of serving the Lord, and the church began to grow in earnest. Each new trial brought new people into the Kingdom.

The Lord touched many other lives through

healing and transformation. The church was able to start two daughter churches, begin a Christian school for children, and have a significant ministry in a center for people with disabilities. The Lord took people from the lowest of sinful conditions and transformed them into mighty workers for the Kingdom, demonstrating again that it is God's power that makes the difference, and that often the highest peaks in ministry are made possible only by the deepest valleys.

Toni and his family had been in Recife for about eight years, and for the last four of them Toni had been supervising the work in a brand-new part of Brazil—Salvador, Bahia, some 16 hours away. God had abundantly blessed both the church and their family, adding a third child, this one a son, Abrão. In spite of the great success they were enjoying in Recife, however, they sensed that the church was in need of a new pastor, and that the Lord was going to be leading them in a new direction. Toni wanted to move to Salvador, Bahia, to pastor on the district where he was serving as superintendent, but he resolved to wait on the Lord.

One day Stephen Heap, missionary director for Brazil, called Toni and asked him to pray about an assignment he had for him. He didn't tell Toni what the assignment was; he merely asked Toni to pray about it. Toni prayed and surrendered his will to the Lord. The Lord directed him to say yes to whatever proposition Stephen had for him, because that was His will for Toni's life. In his heart, Toni was still hoping to be allowed to serve in Salvador, Bahia.

A week later, Stephen called back to give a

name to his proposition. It was São Paulo. Toni was shocked. When he told Lili, she was reluctant, to say the least. It was the last place in the world they would have chosen to go, but the Lord reaffirmed to them that this was where He wanted them to be.

There was a church in the Jabaquara area of São Paulo, near the downtown airport, that was struggling with only 15 or so regular attenders. They needed a pastor, and God had chosen Toni for the task. So in May 1995, with fear and trepidation, the Leão family left their comfortable church running 150 in attendance to start all over again in the high-rise jungle that is São Paulo.

* * *

Toni turned the key to lock up the Jabaquara church as another noisy jet rumbled overhead. Lili, Camila, Margore, and Abrão were already waiting for him in the car. Walking down the steps, he looked out at the view of the city afforded by church property. It wasn't much, but it was home, and they had come a long way to get here.

Toni smiled at Lili as he started the car, and she smiled back. Together and with the Lord, they would make it. No doubt there are other trials and struggles in store for us, Toni thought, but they could be faced victoriously. Truly blessing is found on the other side of burden, and often the greatest trials lead to the greatest of triumphs.

4

Got Any Rivers You Think Are Uncrossable?

The Nilopolis Church of the Nazarene

RIO DE JANEIRO—if you are like most people, that name conjures up images of the long, beautiful beaches of Copacabana and Ipanema and the fantastic, multicolored costumes of the annual pre-Lenten party called Carnival. Perhaps the words of an old song by Tom Jobim titled "The Girl from Ipanema" just came to your memory. You may have even seen pictures of the giant statue of Jesus, called *O Cristo Redentor* (*Christ the Redeemer*), which watches over the city; or the large rocky hill called Pão de Açucar (Sugar Loaf), from which visitors can get a panoramic vista of city and beach alike.

But if that is all you know of Rio, then you really don't know Rio.

Those beaches that are often a mecca for tourists teem with drug users and prostitutes by night. Carnival, which seems so appealing in the brief newscasts seen by the rest of the world, is really a celebration of carnal passion and spiritism. High above the city on Sugar Loaf Mountain, you can still make out the crowded favelas, endless mazes of small, primitive concrete dwellings that many of Rio's inhabitants call home, though the odor of the open sewers and the masses of garbage left to rot in the sun are thankfully hidden from you.

It is in this Rio, the Rio of need and darkness rather than the Rio of glamour and artificial light, that the Church of the Nazarene has found its home.

Far from the tourist beaches and palaces of power that make up the downtown area of Rio de Janeiro (pronounced in Brazil as HEE-oo dee zhah-NAY-roo) is a tired-looking bedroom community called Nilopolis. Like many other such communities surrounding Rio, the area has seen better days. Graffiti graces many of the buildings' walls. On the street are various items of trash or food that society has cast off as useless, perhaps even a few people who fit that description as well. A few horses roam the streets, looking for food in the open garbage pits. However, as in many other communities surrounding the city, in Nilopolis you will find the Church of the Nazarene, and you will find lives being changed.

If you want to visit the Nilopolis church on a Sunday evening, the time of the largest worship service in Brazil, you will need to arrive early. The church is always filled to capacity, and latecomers are forced to sit in the aisle, stand in the back, or even participate in the service from the outside by looking in through the open windows that line the sanctuary. And the church is still growing. In fact, it is the fastest-growing Evangelical church in the area.

What is it that attracts people to this rather unassuming building and its equally unassuming pastor? Love. The church in Nilopolis is a church committed to reaching out and meeting needs wherever it can find them. And it finds them in many different places.

The pastor of the Nilopolis church, and incidentally one of the two Nazarene district superintendents in the state of Rio de Janeiro, is Pedro Paulo Ferreira Matos, himself a story of the transforming grace of God. Pastor Pedro Paulo was saved in a Church of the Nazarene after having grown up with that mix of Roman Catholicism and African spiritism that is so common in Brazil. He grew up thinking of the church as a place one went on weekends, but a place that had little or no impact on the day-to-day lives of hurting people. Then God called him into the ministry later in life while he was working at a children's camp in Serra Negra. And God gave him a vision for a holistic ministry and for a church that was always open and always willing to help in any way it could.

This vision has brought many people into the church, people like Agatha Cristian. This bright young lady is a leader in her youth group who works in the ministry the church has to hearing impaired individuals. Though only 15, she is already in college and studying in the theological extension program of the Nazarene seminary in Brazil so that one day she can fulfill a mission call on her life.

Though Agatha was raised in a Christian home, she became a Christian herself only through a great tragedy, a tragedy that also brought her to the Nilopolis church. When her father committed suicide, the pastor took the time to pray with two confused and hurting young girls who met a God of compassion face-to-face. Through that meeting, Agatha's life was changed, and she has committed that life to being an agent through whom God can change the lives of others.

Like many of the urban areas of the world, Rio de Janeiro suffers from the scourge of drugs, mostly cocaine and marijuana (called *maconha* in Brazil). Many of the members of the Nilopolis church are testimonies to how God can change a life devoted to drugs into a life devoted to Him. The church even has a special ministry called SOS Rescue, which is conducted by former drug addicts and dealers and aims to rescue people from the drug-oriented life.

Jean Dias de Silva is one such individual. Though still a young man, only 21 years old, he has seen his share of the underside of life. When he was 10, Jean found out that his father used drugs, and from then on he knew he was fated to be involved himself. Though he had some church contact when he was 11, he ran away from it because of the tremendous weight he felt on his shoulders. At age 12 he began using marijuana, and at 14 he added cocaine to his list of addictions.

From then on, all of Jean's life revolved around drugs. He smoked marijuana and sniffed cocaine until sometimes he would be stoned for three days straight. When a friend of his became manager of a *"boca de fumo"* (literally, "a mouth of smoke," a place that sells drugs), Jean became his right-hand man.

One day Jean was caught using some of the drugs he was supposed to sell and was severely beaten by the members of the drug cartel in which he was involved. With nowhere else to turn, Jean prayed to God and said that if He would get him out of this situation, then he would become a Christian. Five minutes later he was rescued by the police.

Jean didn't fulfill his vow right away and somehow managed to get a job selling drugs again. Finally, after narrowly escaping another situation that would have surely gotten him killed, he decided once and for all to come to church. He entered the Church of the Nazarene one Sunday evening, and a group of former drug addicts were giving their testimonies. When the invitation was given, Jean was the first person at the altar. In an instant, God delivered him from both his sin and the bondage of drugs, taking away a desire so strong that Jean had thought it inescapable.

Through a miracle of God's grace, Jean is attending the university, even though his drug use in school had caused him to fail 10 subjects and made it difficult for him to learn anything at all. He also serves as the local Nazarene Youth International (NYI) president of the Nilopolis church and is studying in the seminary extension program in Rio—yet one more miracle of God's transforming grace.

Another story of grace in progress is the story of Suzie. Like Jean, Suzie was heavily involved in the drug culture but at an even deeper level. All her brothers were involved with drugs, and she had a nephew who was a dealer. So when Suzie was offered the job as financial manager for the drug cartel in the favela Dona Marta, she accepted. She accepted despite the fact that everyone who had held this job before her had been killed.

Through the consistent, though often rejected, contact of a member of the Nilopolis church working with a medical clinic in Dona Marta, Suzie came in contact with the Church of the Nazarene. This worker made Suzie her special project, and every time she went to treat Suzie's asthma, she would tell her that her life had value and that God loved her.

Suzie couldn't believe that message, however. Then one of the other dealers with whom she worked told her that he had been attending a church. He had decided that this drug-oriented life they were living was not the right thing to do. He advised Suzie to find a real job and quit using drugs.

Suzie tried, but the appeal of the drugs was just too strong, and she was back in the business. Finally she was able to get out and find a job working in a parking garage. She was not able to quit using drugs, however, and they maintained a firm grip on her life.

Then one day she found out that her nephew, of whom she was very fond, had been brutally beaten and killed by the police. She went to his house, and the gore of the scene shocked even her, who had seen many violent scenes in her life. She then allowed this Nazarene clinic worker to take her to church. Finally, at a winter church camp in July 1995, Suzie finally accepted that the Lord loved her and turned her life over to Him.

Suzie has come a long way, but she is still working through the implications of what life in Christ means to her. Her story, like many of our stories, is a story in progress. Pray for Suzie and the others like her, that God will ground them firmly in their faith and that they will be able to resist the temptation to return to their old way of life. As painful as it is to admit, such things do happen, but they are part of the risk you take when you allow yourself to be a vehicle of grace.

There are many other such testimonies in the Nilopolis church, testimonies of deliverance from drugs and deliverance from other things as well. In helping to deliver people from poverty, the Nilopolis church in 1995 gave out over 40,000 bowls of soup. Members of the church have helped people find jobs and have seen wholesale transformations of lives.

One of the pastors of the church, José Carlos, is an ex-convict who found the Lord and now leads a very successful prison ministry along with his wife. The church also has adoption services, volunteers who work in a medical clinic, and a host of other ministries to which the members of the church devote their time and their money. And God has blessed the church in such a way that it has never lacked for funds in its eight-and-a-half-year history, despite the fact that many of members are young people with very small incomes.

God is building His kingdom in Rio de Janeiro through churches like the Nilopolis Church of the Nazarene. He builds it on the foundation of sacrifice and transformed lives, held together with the mortar of love and the bond of the Holy Spirit.

So the next time you see pictures of the statue of *Christ the Redeemer* or hear about that exotic locale that the rest of the world knows as "Rio," remember to pray for the city. Remember, too, that though it is a place often associated with vacations, it is also a place where God is at work.

5

Called from the World and Its Idols to Flee

The Pilgrimage of Nelo Lucas de Jesus

NELO LUCAS DE JESUS GREW UP on the street. It was his choice, really. He could have stayed in the tiny room that his mother and whatever man she happened to be living with at the time called home. But with 10 children, a 9-foot-by-12-foot dwelling can get a little crowded. Add to that the fact that it might collapse during any of the rainstorms to which Rio de Janeiro is accustomed, and it was better to live on the street.

Life in Baixada Fluminense, one of the poorest favelas in Rio, was, and still is, very hard. Nelo spent most of his days begging for food or money and hiding from the police. When he was old enough, he would try to go to school a few days a week when he could afford the time. At night he would sleep on Copacabana beach or Ipanema or even on a bus. It would not matter to him where he slept. One place was very much like another, just as one day was very much like the next.

Occasionally Nelo would go to restaurants and beg food from the managers and patrons. On those rare occasions when someone took pity on him, he had a hot meal. More often he would be treated harshly, and one time a waiter had even beat him over the head with a glass. And even people's kindness could have an ugly face. At one restaurant, Nelo's family was given a hot meal; but after eating it, they all became very ill and had to go to the hospital because the food was spoiled.

During Carnival, or whenever it became politically expedient to show that Rio was a city of sophistication, the police would clear the streets of beggars and other "undesirables." When this happened, Nelo and his brothers would have to run back home and hide. His family all crowded together in their little shack, thinking that even that place was better than prison or a poorhouse.

Once, Nelo and his family were caught by the police and turned over to a poorhouse. They were all separated, and as they figured, the conditions there were worse than on the streets. Sand was softer to sleep on than cement, and on the street they at least had a chance of getting a hot meal. There at the poorhouse they had to stand in long lines for hard, stale bread and water. On the street they were free. The poorhouse was just another word for a prison.

Nelo's mother finally managed to lie her way out of the poorhouse by claiming to be needed by another relative. The police let her and the rest of the family go, warning her to stay off the street; but unfortunately there was nowhere else to go.

Now and then Nelo and his brothers would

beg in front of the Roman Catholic church. Some people would give them money, but others would just give them a piece of paper with some words about a man named Jesus. Nelo usually threw those away because the words didn't make any sense to him, and he couldn't eat the paper.

Given these crowded, cruel, and hopeless conditions, many people who lived on the street turned to theft and violence in order to survive, and drugs or alcohol in order to escape. Given her hopeless life, Nelo's mother had turned to spiritism.

Nelo grew up in an environment of low spiritism. His mother involved him in the spiritist ceremonies, and he had even played the drums in a couple of them before he reached the age of 10. Nelo could not remember a time when his mother did not have wild fits as the spirits tried to possess her. Apparently she was not a very good receptor for the spirits, but she could not afford the spiritist ceremony in which one learned to receive them properly. So she continued to suffer greatly.

Nelo's mother turned to drink to escape the torment of the spirits who would possess her. She would spend as much time drunk as she could, and Nelo and his brothers were always ashamed of her. No matter where she was, at the market, at home, or on the street, she would be gripped by terrible convulsions and fits of shouting, always making a spectacle of herself. This was life for Nelo and his family until God brought them into contact with Dona Aurora.

Nelo's family met Dona Aurora because she had a well, and they learned that she would give water away to people who needed it. Dona Aurora gladly gave Nelo's family all the water they wanted. And while they were drawing it from her well, she would talk to them about a God who loved them, and she would invite them to church. There were even times when she offered the family something to eat, and she would spend the whole time while they were eating talking about Jesus.

After a while, all this talk about God became very boring for 12-year-old Nelo. Dona Aurora was very insistent, and she talked about only one thing. It got to the point that Nelo dreaded having to go and get water from her because he knew that he would have to listen to her talk about God. However, he had to go because it was the only place from which his family could obtain water.

Finally, Dona Aurora had insisted so much that the family agreed to accept her invitation to go to her church, if only for the chance that it might make her stop talking about God. Dona Aurora was very pleased and told them that Jesus would solve all their problems. Nelo had his doubts.

Church was much different from the spiritist centers that Nelo was used to. These people seemed very friendly, and the preacher talked a lot about this Jesus whom Dona Aurora seemed to know so well. Finally, the preacher gave an invitation for anyone who wanted to change his or her life to come to Jesus. Nelo's mother turned to him and the five brothers who were with him and said, "Let's go. It certainly can't make matters any worse."

Nelo's mother went down to the front, and the preacher laid his hand on her. In that instant she fell down in a fit. She got up screaming and ran out of the church. Nelo and his brothers were very frightened, but some of the church members came to try to comfort them. The pastor said from the pulpit that God would bring this woman back, and the rest of the church then lifted their voices in prayer for this obviously distressed woman.

After 10 minutes of prayer, Nelo's mother returned. The preacher laid his hand on her, rebuked the unclean spirit in her, and suddenly a new calm settled over her shaking figure. At that moment Jesus became Lord to her and freed her from the spirits and from alcohol.

Nelo's family changed. He began to learn more about this Jesus and eventually accepted Him as his own Savior. His real father saw the change in Nelo's mother and built a small but nice house for her and her family. She got a job, and Nelo and his brothers were able to attend school regularly. The entire family came to accept that a God who could change their lives so dramatically was truly God indeed.

Through the outreach ministry of the Mesquita Church of the Nazarene, Nelo's family began attending there. It was there that God called Nelo, at the age of 16, to be a pastor.

Nelo had no desire to be a pastor, so he decided that he could be a good Christian and be a layman. But God gave him no peace in that decision. He began to run from the call and also from the Lord. It took almost 10 years for him to come back and accept the fact that pastoring was the Lord's will for his life.

When Nelo accepted the call to ministry, Pastor Amadeu took a special interest in him, discipling him and helping to train him for the pastorate. Nelo also attended the Nazarene seminary extension program in Rio, which was conducted by Pastor Amadeu and his wife. These were times of growth and challenge. When Nelo finished his preparations, God called him to start a church.

"Where should this church be?" Nelo asked of God.

"In the Austin area of Rio," God replied.

Nelo knew of that area. It was where his wife's family lived. As far as he knew, there weren't many Evangelical churches there, so the area was a good place for a church. "Where should we hold the services?" Nelo asked further.

"In your wife's family's house," came the surprising reply.

At this point, Nelo felt it his duty to inform God how inopportune His choice was. After all, both Nelo's mother-in-law and his father-in-law were alcoholics, they were staunch Roman Catholics, and Nelo's father-in-law bore nothing but hate for Evangelicals. In fact, he had just discovered that Nelo, the man who had married his daughter, was an Evangelical, and he was angry beyond belief. It was not exactly the most perfect environment in which to start a church. Still, God's call was firm, and Nelo had to obey.

Just after he had made the decision to contact his wife's family about starting the church, Nelo's father-in-law suddenly died. When he contacted the rest of his wife's family about starting the church, they said, "If this house is where God wants you to start your church, then you must do it. Who are we to argue with God?"

It was 1992 when Nelo began the church in a small 9-foot-by-6-foot veranda. Nobody came to the first service. Within three months, however, there was no longer room enough in the entire house to fit in everyone who wanted to come. The people then started to raise money so that they could build their own church. With a little help from Alabaster, the congregation was able to build a new facility, and that is where they worship today.

Rev. Nelo knows the power of God to change lives. He also knows that there are many lives in Rio that need to be changed. God brought him from the street to salvation, and now he wants to be a vehicle through which He can work to bring that same transformation to others.

6

Faith Is the Victory

The Testimony of Ivonildo Teixeira As Told to Tim Crutcher

MY NAME IS IVONILDO TEIXEIRA. I am the pastor of the Church of the Nazarene in Itapua, Brazil, and district superintendent of the Espírito Santo District. I have a wonderful wife, Monica, and two daughters—Samantha and Talita.

When I was 16 years old, I attended a youth camp where I had my first experience with Jesus Christ. I had arrived at that camp with my heart very empty. I was a kleptomaniac and had stolen from many people, including my father. But in that camp the Lord got very close to me, and He did something in my heart that I never imagined possible.

That day I had the conviction that my sins were forgiven, and I had the assurance that I was a child of God. I sensed the presence of the Holy Spirit taking control of my heart, and I gave myself over to Him. I don't know if this happens to everyone, but that day when Jesus saved me, I believe He also sanctified my heart. The proof of that is that the problems I had had with kleptomania were eliminated from my life. From that day on I didn't take something that wasn't mine, and to me this was the proof that the Holy Spirit had done something in my life. That very day when the Lord saved and sanctified me, He gave me a strong love for the lost and a call into the ministry of the Word.

Two years later, God was talking to me about correcting my life and making restitution to the people I had robbed from in the past. I didn't have peace in my heart, and it was difficult to say that I was a true Christian, knowing that I still owed people.

At that time I didn't know how I could go about making amends. I didn't have any money, any means to make money, and I especially didn't have the courage to face the people I had robbed and make amends. But the Holy Spirit gave me courage, and He gave a job and the opportunity to make enough money to pay the people back.

I went back, person by person, to each one I had robbed in order to make things right. To all the people I contacted I would tell the story of Zacchaeus, and then I would make the restitution. All totaled, there were about 20 people. Undoubtedly, the hardest one to make amends with was my father.

My father was always violent, and he did not seem to know how to communicate with his children. He would yell at us; and when we were late in getting home, we would be whipped. The many terrible scenes I had seen in my home had erected in my heart a great barrier between my father and me. Yet, of all the people from whom I had stolen, my father was the one most hurt by it.

Finally, I had gone to all the people to make amends except my father. Knowing this was something I had to do, I consecrated myself to God and asked Him for grace and strength so that I could face my father.

On the day I decided to make amends with my father, I entered into his bedroom to find him counting money. My father really liked to count money. That was always a problem in his life. And now I had to go and confess to him a crime that was related to his money.

I closed the door, though I don't know where I found the strength to do it, and I started to tell my father the story of Zacchaeus. He just kept right on counting his money. "I know that story," he said, refusing to look at me.

"Father," I said, "I want you to hear this story."

"I'm listening," he said.

I finished the story and asked him, "Do you know why I came here to be with you and tell you the story of Zacchaeus?" He said no. "Father," I said, "just like Zacchaeus had to make restitution to the people he had wronged, I've come here to make right something with you."

All of a sudden he looked at me and said, "What are you trying to tell me?"

I took a deep breath and continued. "Do you remember many years ago when you would notice that money was missing from your pockets or your wallet or your dresser, and you didn't know who it was who would come in and get your money?" He nodded his head yes. I said, "Dad, I was the one who was stealing your money."

At that moment I didn't know what to expect. I thought he would do something to me. I thought he would beat me, hit me on my head, or maybe even use the gun he kept in his room and shoot me. Money was something that was very important to my father, and he was always a moralist, especially when it came to money. That one of his sons would admit to stealing money was a terrible shame for him.

"Dad," I continued, "when I was young, I entered the world of taking things that weren't mine. But about 600 miles away from here in a camp in Serra Negra, I met a Jesus Christ who has changed my life. He has forgiven my sins, and He has told me that I need to go back and make restitution. He spoke to my heart and told me that I should come and talk to you to confess to you my sin and correct my life before you."

All of a sudden, that person whom I remember as always being very hard and strong began to cry. He started coming toward me, and he opened his arms and embraced me, crying. He said, "Son, I forgive you."

"Father," I replied, "I need your forgiveness. I want to make restitution of the things that I should. I don't even remember how much it was that I stole from you those many years ago, but the Holy Spirit helped me over a period of time to save some money, a considerable amount. I have that money with me here, and I want to give that money to you."

"I don't want it," he said.

I insisted, "You *must* want it."

He was still adamant. "No, Ivonildo, there is no way I can take that money."

I said, "Dad, if you don't take this money, my restitution won't be complete."

After I insisted for a long time, he finally took the money in his hands. Then he looked at me and said, "If this is my money, I can do with it what I want." I nodded my head in agreement. "Since it's mine, I'm going to do with it what I want." He handed the money back to me. "Take this money," he said. "Take it as a present from me to you. I'm sure the Lord will show you what you need to do with it."

That was my last act of restitution, and right then I felt as if a tremendous weight had been lifted from my back. I could look at people with a clear conscience now because the Holy Spirit had done a tremendous work in my heart. I went to the Nazarene seminary in Campinas, Brazil, when I was 19 and shared my testimony with everyone I could.

The four years I spent there were years of great growth for me. I learned much, both from what the professors taught and what they lived. I owe a special debt of gratitude to Chuck and Roma Gates, without whom I would not be the minister I am today.

On seminary graduation night, all the other seminary students knew where they were going to minister, but I didn't know where the Lord wanted me to go. It wasn't because I lacked invitations. Several churches in Brazil had invited me to be their pastor. I even had an invitation from my brother who lives in the United States to go there and study for a while. But I didn't feel that God was in that.

That last night I knelt down and asked God to speak to my heart. *Lord,* I prayed, *with the same conviction that I know You saved me and called me to be a pastor, I need to know now where You want me to be a pastor.* That night I dreamed of a map of Brazil. There were no names on that map but one, located in the southeast of Brazil. It was the name of a state that has the most beautiful name of all the states in Brazil—Espírito Santo (Holy Spirit). Its capital also has a very beautiful name—Vitória (Victory). In obedience to that vision, I got my suitcase, my only belonging, got onto the bus, and went to the state of Espírito Santo.

Something tremendous happened in that state. Although I was given a salary of only about $100 a month, I wasn't worried. I believe that the God who is able to direct our lives is also able to provide our daily bread. For my first few days in the city I stayed in the home of some believers I had met there. By faith I rented a house at 9 Guyana Street, on the beach in Itapua, a suburb of Vitória. Today that house rents for $800-900 per month, and I still don't know why the owner was willing to rent to me, but he did.

On March 18, 1984, we had the first service in that house with 18 people present. At the end of that month, we had enough money to pay the rent on that building. From that time on we never lacked funds to pay the rent on that church. One of the names for God is Yahweh Yireh, the God who provides.

Two months later we were averaging 30 people in attendance, and we were in need of a building of our own where we could worship. One Sunday morning, Amadeu Teixeira (my pastor, brother, and district superintendent) was preaching about Christian stewardship and the theme "To give is to live." He preached for two or three hours, but everyone listened attentively. When he went to sit down, a man at the back of the church stood up.

The man held up $5 and an inexpensive watch. "Pastor Ivonildo," he began, "I would like to help buy the property for the church. I don't have a lot, but I have a watch in my hand and about $5 in my pocket. I would like to give these two items to help us buy our first property."

When I saw the Holy Spirit at work in that man's heart that morning, it touched my own heart. I stood up and told the people that the Holy Spirit had asked me to pledge one month's salary, about $300. All of a sudden women started taking off their earrings and giving them as an offering. Men started taking off gold necklaces, rings, and bracelets.

I had never seen anything like it in my life. No one had suggested that the people give their jewelry to the Lord, but the people understood that to give is to live. Men started pledging money. When it was all through, that group of 30 adults and children had given enough to purchase property worth $50,000.

It would have been nice if such a momentous event had been the start of other momentous blessings, but that was not to be. By the time we purchased our property, we had 44 members in the church. But because I was a very young leader and wasn't as perceptive as I could have been, some of our people fell into grievous sin, and it decimated our church. From that original group we were reduced to 4 or 5 members.

During that same time my wife lost the baby she had been carrying. A year later our first daughter was born with Down syndrome. We had the feeling that God was on vacation. It was a very painful period of time for us, but I was convinced that I was where the Lord had called me to be. My wife was a great help to me in those times.

In the midst of all the troubles we were having, the Lord spoke to me and said we needed to start building our church on the property we had purchased. So I went before that small group of 15 or so and said, "We are going to build a church."

They laughed at me and said, "You're crazy. Do you understand what's involved in building a church?"

I replied, "No, I don't, but the Lord does. And He is telling me that we need to begin building our building."

Soon thereafter, in October 1986, the telephone rang in my house. It was Stephen Heap, mission director for Brazil, with the news that Pasadena, California, First Church of the Nazarene wanted to send a Work and Witness team to Brazil to help construct a building for a new church. In my heart I cried out, "Alleluia!" because I knew the Lord was at work. Five months later, Steve Heap showed up with a group of 19 members from Pasadena First Church. I didn't know the pastor of that church or any of its members, but God knew them and directed them to help us build our church.

The arrival of those brothers and sisters from California and the construction work they did really made an impact in the neighborhood. Those people who had left our church began to come back. New people started to come, so the church took on a new profile. Praise the Lord for the group from Pasadena, California!

Right during those days, the Lord took our little daughter who had been born with Down syndrome. It was a very sad experience for us but one that taught me the great love the Father has for all His children, no matter what their abilities or appearance. It was a tremendously painful experience for us, but we kept resting in the Lord. Soon thereafter, the Lord gave us another daughter, whom we named Samantha.

From that time on the church really began to grow. Within a few years we were able to plant a daughter church, the second church in Espírito Santo. I believe that this is because the church in Itapua is a very missionary-minded church. From the time we were only a small congregation, we were always generous in giving to God. We've never missed an opportunity to take up an Alabaster, Easter, or Thanksgiving offering.

Eleven years of faithfulness in giving to the missionary efforts of the church have enabled us to grow. In the last two years we have organized two new churches. When our church building starts to get full, we take a group of people and start a new work in a new area because we want to be able to start churches all over our state.

If I wanted to feed my ego, I could put people in the aisles and all around and have the church totally stuffed. But my concern is not for myself or for my denomination but for the kingdom of God. The vision that the Lord has placed on my heart is to expand the church in that entire state. Our goal is to start the church in two new areas this year. Our theme there is "One for All and All for Jesus."

I'm very thankful for what the Lord is doing through my life, and I am aware that I am an eternal debtor to the gospel. I am thankful to God for my wife and the beautiful daughters He has given us. I dream that by the year 2000 we will have 15-20 churches in the state of Espírito Santo and at least 1,000 members. But my main goal is to be a man full of the Holy Spirit, and I have challenged my people to be the same.

I believe that all the situations that the Church goes through are necessary for the growth of the Church. All the projects, goals, and intentions we have are important for the growth of the Kingdom, but the most important things that will distinguish the Church are not buildings and churches, but lives marked by the Spirit of God.

Please pray for us in Espírito Santo. We want our state and city to live up to their names. We want our state to be taken by the Spirit of God, so that we can truly say that we live in Vitória, Espírito Santo, in the victory of the Holy Spirit. Amen.

7

The Song of the Soul Set Free

Sílvia Rodrigues

SÍLVIA'S FIRST MEMORIES were happy ones. Of course, happiness is a relatively simple concept for a five-year-old. Happiness was hearing her mother sing, watching her father read the magazines he collected, and having a television and a refrigerator. It was a comfortable happiness, a happiness that was supposed to last forever. Then *she* came.

Sílvia's mother answered the door to find a young woman looking for a man named José.

"That's my husband," Sílvia's mother responded.

"That can't be," the young lady replied, "because I'm carrying his child." A picture from the wall proved that they were talking about the same man, and from then on Sílvia's world began to crumble.

Mom and Dad began fighting a lot. Dad began to spend more and more time away from home, and Mother began to spend her time with a bottle. When she did leave the house, it was to take Sílvia and her sisters to strange places where people danced around, lit candles, and poured red liquid in front of ugly black statues.

Over the next few years, the spirits associated with those black statues became a part of life in Sílvia's house. Her mother believed that those spirits would eventually bring her husband back to her, that they would give her the son her husband so desperately wanted. But it seemed to Sílvia that all they brought were sickness and suffering. Even Sílvia seemed to suffer, as there would be times when she would experience fainting spells or the inability to move her legs. Such occurrences were infrequent, but they always scared her.

In Mother's calm moments, which were few, Sílvia and her sisters remembered her reassuring them that their grandparents would take care of them. Though she was only eight, Sílvia thought this odd, since her grandparents were dead. But she remembered seeing an old man and an old woman often sitting on the sofa in the living room, so it must be OK. It wasn't until she saw those same two people in a picture on the shelf of a shop that sold items for the occult practice of macumba that she began to be afraid.

With two families to support, Sílvia's father could no longer maintain the middle-class lifestyle to which they had become accustomed. He soon purchased a small plot of land near Campinas. It wasn't much, but it was all he could afford. He built a small wooden shack that became "home" for the next several years, or at least a place for mother to drink while the children found excuses to be elsewhere. In place of the television and refrigerator, Sílvia's mother set up a number of altars, candles, images, and offerings. Happiness became a word used only of memories.

At the tender age of 12, Sílvia decided to live her own life. She would find a job and study for school at night. She would work hard and do something important with her life. What she found, however, were some friends who introduced her to a drink that made her forget about such things as study and work and a smoke that made her realize nothing was all that important. For the next three years, Sílvia's life revolved around smoking, drinking, and finding as many excuses as she could to stay away from that house where her mother lived, that house that always reminded her of death.

When Sílvia wasn't smoking or drinking, she was trying to find ways to humiliate any boys she knew. She determined that all men were like her father and thus deserved only hatred and disrespect. She would play games with them, lead them on, then dump them and move on to the next one. This continued until one of the boys she was leading on tried to rape her. She escaped and swore that she would have nothing to do with men or boys ever again.

At times Sílvia talked to her dead grandmother about her life, trying to convince her to take her away someplace. She knew she was headed nowhere, but she didn't know of any place to go. She even thought about trying to talk to God, but God to her looked too much like the odd old priest at a church she had attended when she was 6, a priest who required you to kneel down and kiss his hands. Such a God, she thought, was no better than the spirits that tormented her mother.

Not long after Sílvia turned 14, her mother, by now almost completely possessed by the spirits she worshiped, began to beat Sílvia and her sisters. She would often do this without provocation and sometimes severely. When Sílvia came home too late after her graduation from school, her mother gave her the worst beating of her life. At this point Sílvia decided that that kind of life was not worth living.

And that's how on April 15, 1971, one day after graduation from school, Sílvia found herself on a deserted bridge overlooking a railroad track somewhere in Campinas. As she stood there, leaning over the railing on the bridge, Sílvia felt her resolve waver. After all, she was 15 now, she thought. That's old enough to do what she wanted to with her life, such as it was.

She wondered what her parents would think when they found her. Maybe it would get them to wake up, stop fighting, and take care of the other children. Maybe it wouldn't. Either way, she wouldn't have to worry about it anymore. She would no longer have to face that hollow in her heart that had been growing for the past 10 years.

Sílvia knew her life was empty, but she didn't know anything else was possible. And everyone she talked to seemed to feel the same way. Everybody, that is, but Nilsa.

Sílvia had known Nilsa for only about a year, but even in that short amount of time Sílvia had learned that there was something different about her. When the rest of the girls went around to the back of the school to smoke or take pills, Nilsa never joined in. When the other girls would be joking in school, Nilsa would be sitting quietly, reading a large black book.

The most disturbing thing about Nilsa, however, was not that she didn't fit into the crowd. It was that she didn't need to. She was the first person Sílvia had met in a long time who actually seemed to be happy. Nilsa knew Sílvia's smile to be a facade, and one day she confronted her about it.

"You need help," Nilsa stated matter-of-factly. "I met a man who changed my life. You should meet him too."

That was not what Sílvia wanted to hear. Even at 15, Sílvia had had enough of men to last her all her life. She didn't know what the answer to her problems was, but she was sure that it had nothing to do with men.

Looking down from that bridge, however, Sílvia found that she wasn't sure about anything. Suddenly she heard a voice that said, "Go to Nilsa's house."

Sílvia looked around but didn't see anyone there. Leaning back over the railing of the bridge, she heard the voice again. Her nerve shaken and her resolve in shambles, Sílvia quickly left the bridge and hopped on the first bus she could find. She didn't care where she was going; she just wanted to get away.

After Sílvia had been on the bus for several minutes, she finally got her bearings. She realized that this bus was the one she often took to get to Nilsa's house. Still numb from her experience on the bridge, Sílvia got off at Nilsa's stop and walked the short distance to her gate. Nilsa was there waiting for her.

"Please introduce me to this man you say can help me" were the first words out of Sílvia's mouth. Nilsa took her inside her house, calmed her down, and introduced her to Jesus Christ. The next week, Nilsa introduced her to her church, the Church of the Nazarene, and Sílvia began a new life with a new family.

The old family, however, was still very much a part of Sílvia's life, and they didn't like her new life very much. Neither her father nor her mother accepted her decision to accept Christ. Sílvia still found herself avoiding going home, though now she spent her time at church instead of at parties or drinking bashes. When she did finally go home after the service on Sunday nights, her mother would often beat her and tell her not to go to church ever again.

For two years Sílvia continued to sneak away from the house and spend as much time as she could at church. For two years her mother continued to beat her. Finally Sílvia talked to her pastor and told him that she could not take it anymore. Her pastor gave her a startling piece of advice.

Sílvia's pastor told her not to come to church. He told her she must respect her mother and her wishes. He told her she should spend her Sundays at home and tell her mother that she loved her.

For Sílvia nothing could have been more difficult. But even though she was a new Christian, she could tell that this was what the Lord wanted her to do. That next Sunday Sílvia stayed home, much to her mother's surprise. To her mother's even greater surprise, Sílvia told her, for the first time she could remember, that she loved her.

At first, telling her mother that she loved her was difficult for Sílvia, because she didn't really feel it. She still felt great resentment and hatred toward her mother, but she knew that she needed to tell her that she loved her. However, Sílvia found that the more she told her mother that she loved her, the more she found the statement to be true. Soon her mother allowed her to go back to church.

Six months later, it was Mother's Day, and Sílvia was going to sing her first special song in a church service. She invited her mother to come, and she did. That day Sílvia's mother encountered Christ and was radically changed. She was delivered from alcohol, smoking, and even from the evil spirits that had plagued her—all at once.

Sílvia and her mother went home that night and broke all the images and altars that had been devoted to spiritism. A few months later, Sílvia's mother discovered she was pregnant again; this time she had a boy.

This event began a chain reaction of transformation in Sílvia's family, and the grace of God began to take over. Within another year, Sílvia's father had accepted Christ and was reconciled to her mother. The woman with whom he had been living off and on for almost 20 years also found the Lord and married a wonderful Christian gentleman. Soon Sílvia's family was enabled to leave their small wooden shack for a nice home in a comfortable neighborhood.

Through all this time, Sílvia suffered an occasional fainting spell or episode of paralysis in her legs. Her family was worried about her, but every time she went to the doctor, they could find nothing wrong. With everything else going so well, Sílvia decided that she wasn't going to let this one thing get her down.

As all this was occurring in Sílvia's life, she began to feel a growing conviction that God was calling her into the ministry. This disturbed her until she finally convinced herself that it was something she should do later in her life. First she would finish her studies, get married, and have a family; then she could afford to prepare for ministry. And so that is what she did.

In Campinas Sílvia met a young, up-and-coming businessman named Rubens Rodrigues. Though he did not seem to share her experience of Christ, he did agree to go to church with her on Sundays. Thinking this would be enough, Sílvia maintained the relationship, and in March 1979 they were married.

Sílvia's first years of marriage were rocky. Having grown up not respecting any man, she had a hard time giving proper respect to her husband. Her husband continued to attend church but never committed himself to Christ, and this made it increasingly more difficult for Sílvia to maintain her spiritual life. Add to this her husband's business troubles, and the environment of the household was very strained indeed. A little over a year after their marriage, Pablo came along.

Sílvia's pregnancy with Pablo was very difficult. He was four weeks late, and the doctors thought him to be dead. When he was born, he had a terrible infection and had to stay in the hospital for a month. The pregnancy also seemed to make Sílvia's fainting spells and occasional paralysis even worse.

The strain of all this on Sílvia and Rubens's marriage was more than it could take. They decided to look for a lawyer who could help them get a divorce. Before that could happen, however, Sílvia found herself having to be rushed to the emergency room several times. Finally, the doctors decided on an exhaustive battery of tests to determine what was wrong. After a month they discovered her problem.

Sílvia's left kidney had swollen to twice its normal size, and her right kidney, which apparently had never functioned, was the size only of a bean. The doctors decided that a delicate and possibly even dangerous surgery to reduce the enlarged kidney was the only option. In light of this, Sílvia and Rubens decided to postpone any action on their divorce.

On August 12, 1981, Sílvia Rodrigues got down on her knees in her hospital room just a few hours before she was scheduled to go into the operating room. She had run from her call to ministry, and she knew it. Her marriage was failing, and she shared responsibility for that. Knowing that she might not live to see the next day, she told the Lord that she would dedicate her life to Him and that she would do so even if He didn't save her marriage.

The surgery went well, and Sílvia recovered much faster than any of the doctors would have anticipated. She talked with her husband about her call to the ministry and about their marriage, and they agreed to give things a fresh start in a new city—Recife in northeastern Brazil.

In Recife, God continued to do marvelous things in Sílvia's life. Her husband finally committed his life to Christ, and God called him into the ministry. She was able to have another child, and when the doctors did an X ray to determine how her kidneys were functioning after that pregnancy, they found *two* normal kidneys, both in perfect working order. Surely God is a God of miracles.

* * *

Rev. Sílvia Rodrigues stepped out of Casa Amarela Church of the Nazarene into the warm Recife night air. Her academic robe was wet with perspiration, but even that couldn't dampen her spirit on this night. It was March 4, 1996, and it was graduation night for the seminary extension program in Recife, of which Sílvia was the director.

It had been a wonderful 15 years since coming to Recife. Her husband, who had become the pastor of Casa Amarela after filling in as a lay worker, was now serving as district superintendent of the work here in the Northeast. And she was enjoying immensely her role in preparing future and present pastors, evangelists, and missionaries to continue to expand the boundaries of God's kingdom in Brazil and beyond.

Sílvia glanced over at a group of graduates who were standing together, each enjoying a piece of graduation cake. Some were already pastoring, at least one was serving as a missionary in a remote area of the interior of Brazil, and still others would be church planters in this next year when they planned to grow their district by 30 percent.

It seemed a daunting chore, but with God, Sílvia knew, all things were possible. God had brought her this far, and she knew He was still at work. She smiled at that thought, and it made her feel like singing.

8

Onward, Christian Soldiers

THE CHURCH OF THE NAZARENE has been in Brazil since 1958, when Earl and Gladys Mosteller were transferred from Cape Verde to begin the work for the church in the university town of Campinas, about an hour north of São Paulo. When they arrived at the docks in the port city of Santos, Josezito Oliveira, a Cape Verdean who had become a Nazarene in his home country, was there to meet them.

Josezito had come to Brazil after his efforts to immigrate to Argentina had been frustrated. He became the pioneer church planter in Brasília when the capital of Brazil was moved there from Rio de Janeiro. The efforts, sacrifices, and prayers of these families laid the important first stones in the foundation of the church in this country.

Other Cape Verdean Nazarenes, Joaquim and Guilhermina Lima, were also instrumental in helping the church get itself established. Joaquim was the first Nazarene elder and the first elected district superintendent in Brazil. His steady and wise leadership early on helped the church develop into what it is today.

Charles and Roma Gates are two other Brazilian pioneers, now directors of Casa Robles (the Nazarene missionary retirement center), whose tireless efforts on behalf of the church in Brazil can be seen in many lives throughout the country. The full effect of their quiet sacrifice and hours of labor will never be known this side of heaven.

Jim and Carol Kratz arrived in Brazil in 1960, and their 29 years of service have left an indelible mark across the country. Jim and Carol pioneered the church in Rio de Janeiro. They mentored many of the church's present-day leaders and completely identified with the Brazilian people. And the men and women whom they have discipled in the faith are now discipling others, and so the kingdom of God advances.

Jim and Carol's son, J. Eldon Kratz Jr., and his family (Kay and Jonathan and David, later adding Kayla) returned to Brazil in 1982. They too have invested their lives in church planting efforts with a passion for the gospel and for the Brazilian people. They pioneered the work in Porto Alegre, the capital of the state of Rio Grande do Sul. In Curitiba the Kratzes found an effective ministry to grieving families by helping them with funeral preparations and offering a comforting word or whatever else was needed. Today they are working in Florianópolis, the capital of Santa Catarina, opening the work of the church in that state.

All across the Church of the Nazarene you will find pastors, leaders, and laypeople who found

Christ or heard their calls to the ministry at summer camps, and Brazil is no exception. Robert and Frances Collins, who arrived in Brazil in 1962, pioneered the camp concept for the denomination in that country with powerful and ongoing results. The Collinses served in Brazil until Robert was wounded by gunshot from a robber in his home in 1994. That miraculous story will have to await its telling in another book.

In Curitiba and Londrina, Rex and Edith Ludwig pioneered new districts, opening up the entire southern region for the Church of the Nazarene. Since 1973 they have continued to labor in a church planting ministry that has borne lasting fruit over the years.

After serving for 26 years in the Cape Verde Islands, Elton and Margaret Wood came to Brazil in 1976 and poured their lives into the students who came through the Brazilian seminary. Today all across Brazil you will find many people who owe much of their spiritual foundation and formation to this wonderful couple.

There have been many others who have invested their lives in Brazil and in the Brazilian people. Stephen and Brenda Heap arrived in Brazil in 1974 and today direct the mission work throughout the country, planning, dreaming, and praying about what the Church of the Nazarene in Brazil could become. Brian and Beryl Adams came to Brazil in 1968 with the Unevangelized Fields Mission. In 1981 they became Nazarene missionaries and presently teach at the seminary. Others have come for shorter periods of time, and they too have had a part in planting the seeds of God's kingdom.

Today there is a strong Church of the Nazarene in Brazil, but none of the present strength would have been possible without the past sacrifice. In these pages you have glimpsed just a few of the transformed lives God has added to His kingdom through the Church of the Nazarene. And there is so much more to the story yet to be told.

God is at work in and through the Church of the Nazarene in Brazil. In the last 30 years He has enabled the church to grow from a fledgling work into a strong, healthy network of districts and churches. The church is rapidly becoming a mature church, one strong enough and well grounded enough to face the challenges ahead of it.

Statistics must always be used with care, because numbers never tell the whole story, but they can help to round out the picture of Brazil given in the previous pages. Today in Brazil there are more than 16,000 Nazarenes in 182 churches on 14 districts. All but one of those districts is led by a Brazilian Nazarene. Three hundred fifty students are involved in theological education, most of it by extension from the Seminario Teologico Nazareno Brasileiro in Campinas. As of this writing, there is Nazarene work in 16 of the 26 states of Brazil and also in the Federal District of Brasília.

However, Brazilian Nazarenes are not satisfied with where they are and are praying and working to go even farther. By the year 2000 they hope to have 36,000 members in 600 churches and work in every state in the country.

This growth has been and can only be accomplished because of a commitment to evangelism by the Brazilian church. A glimpse of this can be seen in the stories contained in this book. For the most part, new areas of Brazil are not being opened up by expatriate missionaries. They are being opened up by Brazilian Nazarenes committed to reaching their country for Christ. The six regular districts of Brazil have teamed up in order to plant a church in the capital city of every state by the turn of the millennium. They are backing up that commitment with prayers, personnel, and money.

Sheer numerical growth is not the only sign of strength in the Brazilian church, although it is a very encouraging one. Another equally encouraging sign is that the Brazilian church has committed itself to reach people for Christ outside Brazil. God is mobilizing the Church of the Nazarene in Brazil for mission. There is already one Brazilian couple serving as missionaries in Portugal (Nathanael and Rita Cardoso), and the church has committed itself to providing two more such couples during the next four years. They are even setting up an infrastructure by which they will be able to support these missionaries with Brazilian prayers and Brazilian financial resources.

Inspired by the impact that Work and Witness teams from Point Loma Nazarene College have made on their country, Brazilian young people are beginning to form *Jovens em Missões* (Youth in Mission) for the purpose of getting involved in missions and evangelism on a broader scale. This initiative is still in its earliest stages, but the enthusiasm and commitment of the youth involved give the project great promise.

As encouraging as all these signs are, the Church of the Nazarene in Brazil still faces significant challenges and obstacles to their future. Please make these a matter of prayer as you pray for Brazil.

One of the greatest challenges facing the church in Brazil is the lack of sufficient Holiness literature in Portuguese. With limited financial resources, the church cannot produce enough literature to meet the need of good Portuguese Sunday School material, devotional material, and study material. Pray that God will open doors to meet this great need.

With the increasing number of people involved in Theological Education by Extension in Brazil, another challenge is finding a structure and sufficient resources for the program to meet the needs of the students and give them a high-quality education without increasing the cost.

One of the problems involved in such wonderful growth as Brazil has seen is that the financial support for ministry has a difficult time keeping up with the open doors. General Budget laid the foundation to make such growth possible, but it cannot and should not be the determining factor for all ministry. Pray that the Brazilian Nazarenes will be able to find ways to generate resources within their country and not be confined by ministries dependent upon General Budget money.

As you pray for Brazil, remember, too, the pastors who are pioneering new works in new areas of the country, sometimes a day's travel from the closest other Nazarenes. Pray that the Lord will encourage them in their task and that they will find their strength in Him.

Finally, remember the Nazarenes in Brazil as they battle the dark spiritual forces so prevalent in that country. With spiritism and the occult so openly accepted in many places, the battle can be intense at times. Pray that the Lord will strengthen the believers and assure them that He is more powerful than any other force they might encounter.

God is truly at work in Brazil. It can be seen in the transformed lives who are living testimonies to His grace. It can be seen in the excitement to be found at district gatherings, conventions, and assemblies, where people talk about all the wonderful things God is doing. And it can also be found in the quiet prayers of thousands of Brazilian Nazarenes praying for their country and for the kingdom of God around the world.

The kingdom of God is marching on in Brazil, with the sacrifices of those who have come and now have passed on, with the commitment and fervency of those who are currently engaged in the battle, and, as always, "with the cross of Jesus going on before."